HOW TO LIVE

HOW TO LIVE

*27 conflicting answers
and one weird conclusion*

DEREK SIVERS

HIT MEDIA

Producer: Saeah Lee Wood

How to Live ISBNs:
978-1-99-115230-5 hardcover
978-1-99-115231-2 paperback
978-1-99-115232-9 EPUB
978-1-99-115234-3 PDF
978-1-99-115235-0 mobi
978-1-99-115236-7 mp3
978-1-99-115237-4 m4b

Hit Media
New York, Paris, Hong Kong, Mumbai
hitmedia.com

This is an homage to the book *Sum* by David Eagleman.

CONTENTS

Please read slowly.
One line at a time.

HERE'S HOW TO LIVE:
BE INDEPENDENT.

All misery comes from dependency.
If you weren't dependent on income, people, or technology,
you would be truly free.
The only way to be deeply happy is to break all dependencies.

Most problems are interpersonal.
To be part of society is to lose a part of yourself.
Cut ties with society.
Don't engage.
Don't even rebel, because that's reacting.
Instead, do what you'd do if you were the only person
on Earth.

People think we live in a world of politics, society, norms,
and news.
But none of it is real.
They're just interpersonal drama.
They're the noisy waste product of unhealthy minds.

Crowds are hysterical, and inbreed opinions.
Don't be a part of any group.
Don't take sides on any fight.
Instead of standing out from the crowd, just avoid and ignore
the crowd.
Avoid social media and the zeitgeist.
Its stupidity will infect you.
Don't align with any religion, philosophy, or political stance.
Stay unlabeled and unbound.

Rules and norms were created by the upper class to protect
their privilege — to categorize people into high versus low
society.
None of it applies to you.

Long ago, people had to follow norms to have high social status, otherwise they'd be ostracized and couldn't survive. But now you can survive, mate, and thrive without social status.
So it's both irrational and unwise to follow those norms.

Dogs bark.
People speak.
It doesn't mean a thing.
What they say and do has nothing to do with you, even if it seems directed your way.
The only opinion that matters is your own.
When you know what you're doing, you won't care what anyone else is doing.
When you're indifferent to people's words and actions, nobody can affect you.

Don't believe anything anyone says.
Listen if you want, but always decide for yourself.
Never agree with anything the same day you hear it, because some ideas are persuasively hypnotic.
Wait a few days to decide what you really think.
Don't let ideas into your head or heart without your permission.

Being independent means you can't blame others.
Decide everything is your fault.
Whoever you blame has power over you, so blame only yourself.
When you blame your location, culture, race, or history, you're abdicating your autonomy.

Everyone has their own lives to manage.
Nobody is responsible for you, and you aren't responsible for anybody.
You don't owe anyone anything.

Friends are great at the right distance.
Just like you can't read something if it's pushed up
against your face, or too far away, you should keep your
friends at arm's length — close but not too close.

Have more than one romantic partner, or none.
To avoid emotional dependence, never have just one.
Don't worry about being lonely.
Nothing is more lonely than being with the wrong person.
It's always better to be alone.

You can't be free without self-mastery.
Your past indulgences and habits might be addictions.
Quit a harmless habit for a month, just to prove you can.

When you say you want more freedom from the world,
you may just need freedom from your past self.
You don't see things as they are.
You see them as you are.
Change yourself and you change the world.

Learn the skills you need to be self-reliant.
Learn to drive, fly, sail, garden, fish, and camp.
Learn emergency medical and disaster preparedness.
Assume nobody will help you.

Don't depend on any company, especially not
the big tech giants.
Use only open-source software and open
communication protocols.
Keep your own backups.
Get your own domain.
Run your own server.

Live where you feel most free.
Move symbolically far away from where you grew up.
Living in a foreign place helps make it clear that

this culture's rules don't apply to you.

The best place for self-reliance is a rural off-the-grid home.
Generate your own electricity.
Collect your own water.
Grow your own food.

Or have no home at all.
When you have no home, the whole world is your home.
Be a nomadic minimalist to break dependencies on stuff.
Our hunter-gatherer ancestors thrived by carrying nothing,
then finding or making what they needed.

Be a perpetual traveler, living out of a suitcase.
Move to a new country every few months, never a registered
resident of anywhere.
Spread the different aspects of your life across different
countries to avoid depending on any one country.
Earn multiple passports.
If a country enters into war or makes your life hard, just leave.
To be nomadic is to be a pacifist.

Make friends wherever you go, so that no one place has all of
your friends.

Own your own business with many small customers to avoid
depending on any big client.
Offer products, not a personal service, so your business can
run without you.
Create many sources of income like this.

Don't sign contracts.
Be willing to walk away from anything.

Eventually, you will have done it.
You'll be absolutely free and independent.
It's the ultimate liberation.

Then you can appreciate everything from a healthy distance.
You can appreciate your country from abroad, once it's not
your only option.
You can appreciate family, once they're not forced upon you.
You can laugh at the hysteria of the crowd, and learn from
it too.
You can take sides in a fight, with a smirk.
You can even take responsibility for someone else.

Being fully independent is how to live.

Here's how to live: Commit.

If you've ever been confused or distracted,
with too many options...
If you don't finish what you start...
If you're not with a person you love...
... then you've felt the problem.
The problem is a lack of commitment.

You've been looking for the best person, place, or career.
But seeking the best is the problem.
No choice is inherently the best.
What makes something the best choice?
You.
You make it the best through your commitment to it.
Your dedication and actions make any choice great.

This is a life-changing epiphany.
You can stop seeking the best option.
Pick one and irreversibly commit.
Then it becomes the best choice for you.
Voilà.

When a decision is irreversible, you feel better about it.
When you're stuck with something, you find what's
good about it.
When you can't change your situation, you change your
attitude towards it.
So remove the option to change your mind.

You think you want more choice and more options.
But when you have unlimited choice, you feel worse.
When you keep all options open, you're conflicted
and miserable.
Your thoughts are divided.
Your power is diluted.

Your time is thinly spread.
Indecision keeps you shallow.
Get the deeper pleasure of diving into one choice.

The English word "decide" comes from Latin "to cut off".
Choose one and cut off other options.
To go one direction means you're not going other directions.
When you commit to one outcome, you're united and
sharply focused.
When you sacrifice your alternate selves, your remaining self
has amazing power.

Ignore other aspects of your life.
Let go of every unnecessary obligation.
Each one seems small, but together, they'll drain your soul.
Focus your attention on the few things you're committed to,
and nothing else.

When our ancestors shifted from nomadic hunter-gatherers
to settled land developers, human development boomed.
We made massive advances when we stopped moving, and
committed to one place.
Choose your home.
Stay there for good.
Get to know everything about it.
Even if you've lived there for years, hire a local expert and
learn even more about the history, architecture, and areas
you haven't explored.

Find a community of like-minded people.
Don't waste your energy fighting norms.
Trust helps your happiness more than income or health.
Invite your neighbors over for a meal.
Make friends.
Make the effort.
Borrow and lend.
Trust and show you can be trusted.

Let them know they can lean on you because you're here to stay.
They'll reciprocate.

You'll be an inseparable part of your community.
The good relationships you build will build you.
There's no greater strength in hard times.

When you stay in one place, daily life is better.
There's little incentive for businesses to give good service to someone who's only passing through.
But by committing to a community, people treat you better.
The rules are different.
They know they'll see you every week so it's in their best interest to treat you well.
You're more of a friend than a stranger.

The more social ties we have, the happier we are.
The bond of friendship is one of the deepest joys in life.
Notice those words: ties, bond.
These are words of commitment.
We say we want freedom, in theory.
But we actually prefer this warm embrace.

You and your best friends don't decide anew each day whether you're friends or not.
You are friends, without question.
You're committed to each other, even if you've never said so.
That's what's wonderful about it.

When people say you're a person of good character, they mean you're not just good, but consistently so.
You're defined by what you do repeatedly.
Your habits create your character.

Once you decide what's important to you, you know how
your ideal self will act and what your ideal day will be.
So why not act that way and live that day every day?
Commit to your habits to make them rituals.
If it's not important, never do it.
If it's important, do it every day.

Rockets use most of their fuel in the first minute of flight,
to escape the pull of gravity.
Once they get outside that pull, it's effortless.
Same with your habits.
Starting is hard.
The rest is easy.

New habits are what you're trying.
Old habits are who you are.

Commit to one career path.
Build your expertise and reputation over time.
Because you cut off other options, you won't be derailed
by distraction.
Since you're committed, you can't fail.
Even if it takes you years longer than expected, it's not failure
until you give up.

This even goes for technical choices, whether hardware
or software.
Pick one.
Commit to it.
Learn it deeply.
This is much more rewarding than always switching and
searching for the best.

Marry.
Marry someone full of kindness who is committed to putting you in the center of their life.
Marry someone you don't want to change, who doesn't want to change you.
Someone that doesn't punish you for mistakes.
Someone who sees you as your highest potential.
Commit completely.

Falling in love is easy.
Staying in love is harder.
Enthusiasm is common.
Endurance is rare.

Marriage is for getting through the times when you're not in love.
Expect things to get bad.
Your mutual commitment gives you the security to weather the storms, knowing they won't destroy the relationship.
Be loving even when you're not feeling loving.

Commitment gives you peace of mind.
When you commit to one thing, and let go of the rest, you feel free.
Once you decide something, never change your mind.
It's so much easier to decide just once.

Commitment gives you integrity and social bonds.
Commitment gives you expertise and power.
Commitment gives you love and happiness.
Committing is how to live.

HERE'S HOW TO LIVE:
FILL YOUR SENSES.

See it all.
Touch it all.
Hear it all.
Taste it all.
Do it all.
Appreciate this wonderful physical world.

If you knew you'd go blind tomorrow, how intensely would
you look at the world today?
If you knew you'd go deaf tomorrow, how intensely would
you listen?
Fill your senses as if this was your last day on Earth.
One day that will be true.

Maximize your inputs.
See all the places.
Eat all the food.
Hear all the music.
Meet all the people.
Kiss all the beauties.
Be insatiable.

Life is short.
How to experience it all?
Here's the key:
Here's your mission:
Nothing twice.
Never eat the same food twice.
Never go to the same place twice.
Never hear the same thing twice.
Everything only once.

Be systematic.
Follow guides.
"Top Places You Must Visit"
"Greatest Movies of All Time"
"Best Restaurants in Town"
Go through them all.
That's the optimized way to experience the most,
without repetition.

Always forward.
Never back.
Push yourself.
Always be a stranger in a strange land.
But don't rush.
Savor every aspect of everything you take in.
Notice the nuances.

Find places that bombard your senses.
India.
Burning Man.
Festivals.
Museums.
Celebrations.
Funerals.

Skydive.
Scuba dive.
Run with bulls.
Swim with sharks.
Float in space.

How to pay for this wonderful life?
Only two choices.

The bad choice is a travel writer.
Looks glamorous and easy, so everyone tries it.
May be possible, but every rich kid does it for free.

The smart choice is sales.
It will always be valuable.
Learn to sell, and you can go anywhere.
You'll be paid well at any age.
Always in high demand.
Get a job on the road.
Always talking to strangers.
That's what you need.

Simple decisions help avoid repetition.
Don't have a home.
Never sleep in the same place twice.
No kitchen.
No cooking.
Every meal somewhere new.
Never go down a road you recognize.

Simple systems help force change.
Every month, get rid of your existing clothes.
Get new clothes in a new style.
Do this while traveling, so one month your clothes are from
Morocco, next month from Italy, next month from Japan.

This is good for you.
The variation in diet is good for your health.
The new situations are great for your brain.

Never have the same thought twice.
Keep nothing on your mind.
Just take in what's around you now.
Have no expectation of how something should be, or you
won't see how it really is.

How amazing that everything you're doing is both the first
and last time.
The thrill of the first.
The sentimentality of the last.

There will be things you'll love so much you'll want to stay or do them again.
But no.
Remember your mission.

Experience pain, anger, sorrow, and more.
Don't judge them as bad.
Notice how they really feel.

Practice seduction.
Be with a different person every night.
Every lover is different.
Don't allow relationships.
Remember: no repetition.

But after decades of this, you'll need something radically new.
Stay in one place.
Be with one person.
Buy a home.
Raise a baby.
It's terrifying, but if you don't, it will be the one experience you never had.

Here's how to live: Do nothing.

The ten commandments said what not to do.
Most of being a good person is not doing bad.
Don't be cruel or selfish.
Don't lie or steal.
Just do no harm.

People always think they need to do something.
One action creates a problem, fixed by another action, so they
react and counter-act, creating more problems to fix.
All of this can be avoided.
All actions are optional.
You don't have to act or react.
You don't have to do anything.

Criminals justify their crimes by saying they were in a crisis
and had to do something.
People mistakenly say yes to work, people, and places they
don't like, then need to escape to get away from their mistakes.
People make bad decisions because they felt they had to
decide.
It would have been wiser to do nothing.

People destroy relationships with an angry over-reaction.
The metaphors for "blowing off steam" or "venting" are
wrong.
Expressing your anger doesn't relieve it.
It makes you angrier.

Actions often have the opposite of the intended result.
People who try too hard to be liked are annoying.
People who try too hard to be attractive are repulsive.
People who try too hard to be enlightened are self-centered.
People who try too hard to be happy are miserable.

So the best way to live is to do nothing.
Stop all the thinking and doing.
Be still and silent.
No actions and no reactions.
No judgments and no conclusions.
No craving and no fixing.

Change your need to change things.
In your most peaceful moments, your mind is quiet.
You're not thinking you should be doing anything else.
When everything feels perfect, you say, "I wouldn't change a thing."
So, live your whole life in this mindset.

Don't hope.
Hope is wanting things to be different than they are.
Wanting to change yourself is self-loathing.
There's no deeper happiness than wanting nothing.
Desire is the opposite of peace.

Most of what people say and do is unnecessary.
Most talk is just noise.
The English word "noise" comes from "nausea".
Say nothing unless it must be said.

People will appreciate your silence, and know that when you speak, it must be important.
Shallow rivers are noisy.
Deep lakes are silent.

Silence is precious.
Silence is the one thing that all religions have in common.
Silence is the only way to hear quiet wisdom.

Most trouble is caused by action.
No action, no trouble.

Most actions are a pursuit of emotions.
You think you want to take action or own a thing.
But what you really want is the emotion you think it'll bring.

Skip the actions.
Go straight for the emotion.
Practice feeling emotions intentionally, instead of using actions to create them.
You don't need marriage to feel security.
Marriage doesn't make you secure.
You don't need recognition to feel pride.
Recognition doesn't give you pride.
You don't need a beach to feel tranquility.
Places don't make emotions.
You do.

Your whole experience of life is in your mind.
Focus on your internal world, not external world.

When a problem is bothering you, it feels like you need to do something about it.
Instead, identify what belief is really the source of your trouble.
Replace that belief with one that doesn't bother you.
Then the problem is solved.
Most problems are really just situations.

You make decisions to feel forward motion.
But it's a treadmill that takes you nowhere.
When someone asks you to decide, just refuse.
The longer you go without deciding, the more information is revealed.
Eventually, the choice is obvious and made without an agonizing decision.

Just because somebody asked you a question doesn't mean you have to answer it.

Dramatic people are fueled by reactions.
When you stop reacting, they go away.

Same goes for yourself.
Your emotions insist they need you to respond.
When you ignore the urges, they go away too.

Observe yourself.
Your own mind is the best laboratory.
It's also the most private and peaceful place to work.

To be wise, shut out all media and opinions.
No news, no gossip, no entertainment.
Most of it is not worth knowing.

Junk may reach your senses, but don't let it reach your mind.
Don't accept the false stories people tell.
Things are neither good nor bad — they're as neutral as a rock.
When people give opinions, add a question mark.
If they say, "Immigration is bad," change it to, "Immigration
is bad?"
Let the questions drift away, unanswered.

The unintelligent jump to conclusions.
The wise just observe.
Wisdom comes from removing the junk, lies, and obstacles to
clear thinking.
Instead of learning more, get wise by learning less.
Keep an empty head, so you can observe clearly.

The less you do, the more you can see.
Observe and learn.
Watch the world.

Live where nothing is happening.
Move to a quiet place with lots of nature and no ambition.
Doing nothing is normal there.
Walk and appreciate nature for hours a day.

Your life and mind will be tranquil and serene.
Peace is the absence of turmoil.
You won't need the media, the internet, or a phone.
Your cost of living will be hardly more than local eggs
and vegetables.
Doing nothing is the ultimate minimalism.

If you need money, be an investor.
It's the only career where you profit the most by doing
the least.
It should take no more than an hour per month.
The stock market takes money from the active traders
and gives it to the patient.

If an action feels necessary, and you can't let it go, just write it
down for later.
Everything seems more important while you're thinking of it.
Later, you'll realize it's not.

But if it still feels necessary, adjust your time frame.
A year from now, will it be important?
Ten years from now?
Zoom out as far as you need to make it unimportant.
Then you're free of it.

But you may think the world needs you to do something.
That line of thinking makes it upsetting to die.

Let go of feeling needed.
Let go too soon instead of too late.
The world doesn't need you.
You're relieved of your duty because soon you won't exist.
Do nothing now to show that life goes on without you.
Be selfless.
Be free.

Doing nothing is how to live and how to die.

HERE'S HOW TO LIVE:
THINK SUPER-LONG-TERM.

In 1790, Benjamin Franklin gifted £2000 to the cities of
Philadelphia and Boston by putting it into a 200-year trust,
and by 1990 it was worth over $7 million.
If you put $2000 into the stock market for 200 years at the
average 8% return, it will be worth over $9 billion.
If you can do $100,000, it will be worth over $483 billion.

Live like this.
Serve the future.
Do small things now with huge benefits for your older self,
your descendants, and future generations.

Actions amplify through time to have a massive impact on
the future.
Let this fact guide your life.
Use a time machine in your mind, constantly picturing your
future self and your great-grandchildren's world.
Act now to influence that time.

The actions are obvious.
Put money in an investment account and never withdraw.
Eat mostly vegetables.
Exercise always.
Get preventative health checkups.
Make time for your relationships.
Do these, yes, but let's look at less-obvious ones.

The biggest challenge is to think long-term when life is
pulling you around.
You need a constant vivid reminder.
So use an age progression filter — the software that takes a
photo of a face and makes it look thirty years older.
Run it on some photos of yourself.

See your elderly face, and take care of that person.
Run it on photos of the people you care for.
Save the results and put them where you'll see them every day.
These future people are your responsibility now.

Imagine your future self judging your current life choices.
When making a decision, ask yourself how you'll feel about it
when you're old.
What would your future self and family thank you for?
Simple actions now will compound to give them a better life.

Delay gratification.
Today's discomfort brings future rewards.
When you have a clear view of the future, you won't mind the
small sacrifice.
You never regret not indulging.

Only spend money on things that do long-term good,
like education.
In other words, never spend, only invest.
The earlier you start, the better, since time is the multiplier.

Many huge achievements are just the result of little actions
done persistently over time.
Cities began with just one building.
Walmart was one little store.
People with incredible skill just practiced every day.
Put $25 a day in your investment account, and in thirty years,
you'll have over a million dollars.

We overestimate what we can do in one year.
We underestimate what we can do in ten years.
If you take up a new hobby at the age of forty, or whatever age
you think is too late, you'll be an expert by the age of sixty.

Be extra-careful of habits that seem harmless.
Imagine each choice continuing forever.
Eat a cookie, and eventually you're obese.
Shop for fun, and eventually you're deep in debt.
When you choose a behavior, you choose its future
consequences.

Thinking of the future doesn't come naturally.
Our hunter-gatherer ancestors had to live moment-to-moment,
so our tendency to focus on today is built into our biology.
But times have changed.
Now the surviving fittest are the ones who plan ahead.

You owe your quality of life to people in past generations.
We say someone is lucky if they are born into a rich family, in a
stable country, full of opportunity.
But that luck was created by the grandparents that moved to
that promising place, then worked hard and saved money for
the next generation instead of spending it themselves.
Make your grandchildren lucky like this.
Move to a place with good values that's headed in the right
direction.

Climate change might make everything between 40° and -40°
latitude quite unlivable, so start getting legal resident status
in a country outside of that, like Canada, New Zealand, or the
Nordics.
These might be the last livable places on Earth.
Make sure your grandchildren will have citizenship.
Be a great ancestor.

Plan your death.
Write your will now.
Make sure your heirs know where everything is, and who to
contact.

Short-term thinking is the root of most of our problems,
from pollution to debt, both personal and global.
Easter Island used to be filled with trees, but early settlers
cut them down, and they never grew back.
Greenland used to have grass, but early settlers let their
sheep graze, and it never grew back.
A few short-term decisions can lead to centuries of destruction.

We treat the future like a garbage dump.
We dump our debts, pollution, junk, and responsibilities on
the future, as if it's a problem solved.
It's the most psychopathically inconsiderate thing we do to
our children, since it's their world, not ours.

Your future self is depending on you.
Your descendants are depending on you.
Our future generations are depending on us.
Use the compounding amplifier of time.
Thinking super-long-term is how to live.

HERE'S HOW TO LIVE:
INTERTWINE WITH THE WORLD.

We're all cousins.
Everybody on Earth, no matter how far apart, has a
surprisingly recent common ancestor.
Go meet your family in the Middle East, in Asia, in Africa, in
the Americas, and in Europe.
Understand that there is no "them".
It's just "us".
Feel those connections.

You have kindreds scattered around the world.
People who are weird like you are spread out everywhere.
One of the best feelings in life is to meet someone who grew
up in an opposite culture but has your same humor, thoughts,
or taste.

If you want a successful network of connections, what matters
is not how many people you know but how many different
kinds of people you know.
Building relationships worldwide brings more opportunity,
more variety, and more chance for circumstance.

Moving across the world makes you smarter, because you stop
thinking you're always right.
Those who shout, "my country is the best!" are those who
have never left.
In Icelandic, the word for "idiot" means "one who has never
left home to journey abroad".
Only idiots think they're always right.

You can't see your own culture while you're inside of it.
Once you get out and look back, you can see which parts of
your personality actually come from your environment.

Traveling makes you better at communicating, since you can't assume familiarity, and must speak simply and clearly.
You'll get used to speaking with people of different religions, worldviews, and communication styles.
You'll know when to be formal, when to joke, when to reference tradition, and when to swear.

How far should you travel?
Look to nature's example of floating dandelion seeds and sticky burrs.
Plants and trees spread their seeds as far as possible.
And so should you.
Spread your DNA worldwide.
Not just your biological DNA, but the other things that make you who you are: your ideas, values, and relationships.

To live a full and rewarding life, intertwine yourself with the world.

Move somewhere far away.
Plan to stay.
Bring no baggage.
Leave your expectations and certainties behind.

This new strange place will feel wrong.
You'll find fault in most of its ways.
The clothes you arrive in are not suited for its climate.
The beliefs you arrive with are not suited for its culture.
Replace both with locally-made clothes and beliefs.
Eventually, they'll fit you well.

Ask questions until you understand why things are the way they are.
Culture is often historical.
Like a person's outlook on life is shaped by what they've been through, a culture's values are shaped by its recent history.
Learn the local mindset.

Don't ask how "they" do things.
Ask how "we" do things.
That small difference is important.
This is your new home.

Once a place really feels like home, move somewhere new.
Pick a confusing or scary place that you don't understand.
Repeat the process.
Make it your home.
Try to make the connection official by getting visas, residency, and citizenship.
Do this until no part of the world feels foreign.

From Brazil, learn to live in the present, and embrace every stranger as a friend.
Leave before you forget about the future.

From Germany, learn rationality and directly honest communication.
Leave before you start scolding strangers.

From Japan, learn deep consideration for others, social harmony, and intrinsic perfection.
Leave before you get so considerate that you can't express yourself or take action.

From China, learn pragmatism and the multi-generational mindset.
Leave before you get superstitious or prioritize social status.

From France, learn idealism and resistance.
Leave before you oppose everything in theory.

From America, learn expressive rebellious individualism.
Leave before thinking you're the center of the world.

From India, learn to improvise and thrive in complexity.
Leave before feeling a divide between what's inside versus
outside your circle.

In all cultures, avoid the madness of the crowd.

Have a child with someone from Asia, Africa, the Americas,
and Europe.
The greater the variety of races, the better.
Raise your kids with many influences, many parents, and
many families.
Help raise other people's kids for the same reason.
Make voluntary families.
Make wider and inclusive families.

Some say "blood is thicker than water," as if only your
immediate relatives have blood.
But everyone has blood, and you're related to all of them.

If you eventually need a permanent home, choose the place
you'd want to be if everything goes wrong.
Choose a culture that values what you value.

When you die, you leave behind your genes and ideas.
The atoms in your cells will disassemble and become plants,
animals, dirt, and oceans.
Bits of you will eventually become part of the whole world.
The way to live is to spread your seeds widely before you die.

Here's how to live: Make memories.

You recently had a day, or even a month, that you can't remember.
If I asked what you did then, you couldn't say.
There was nothing unusual about it.

What if you have many more of those?
What if, when you're older, you can't recall entire years?
If you can't remember something, it's like it never happened.
You could have a long healthy life, but if you can't remember it, it's like you had a short life.
What a horrible way to live.

When you're young, time goes slowly because everything is new.
When you get older, time flies by, forgotten, because you're not having as many new experiences.

You need to prevent this.
Monotony is the enemy.
Novelty is the solution.

Go make memories.
Do memorable things.
Experience the unusual.
Pursue novelty.
Replace your routines.
Live in different places.
Change your career every few years.
These unique events will become anchors for your memories.

Remember them all.
Document everything, or you'll eventually forget it.
Nobody can erase your memories, but don't lose them through neglect.

Journal every day.
Write down your activities, thoughts, and feelings for future reference.

Video everything.
Compile and edit them, so they're appealing to watch.

To enjoy your past is to live twice.
Nostalgia links your past and present.
Nostalgia protects against stress and boredom, and improves your mood.
Nostalgia makes you more optimistic, more generous, more creative, and more empathetic.
Nostalgia is memories minus the pain.
Being nostalgic makes you less afraid to die.

Turn your experiences into stories.
A story is the remains of an experience.
Make your stories entertaining, so people like to hear them.
By telling good stories, your memories can last longer, because people will echo them back to you occasionally, or ask you to tell them again.

Make a story for the things you want to remember.
Never make a story for the things you want to forget.
Let those disappear with time.

Your memories are a mix of fact and fiction.
Your story about an experience overwrites your memory of the actual experience.
So use this in your favor.
Re-write your past.
Embellish adventures.
Disempower trauma.
Re-write your stories into whatever works for you.
Remember only what you want to remember.
You have the right to reframe.

Summarize a painful time into a tiny story — under a minute.
Tell this belittled version a few times to make it stick.
This is the version you'll remember — stripped of pain and power.

How you feel about anything is based on how you look back at it.
Your memory is influenced by how you feel now.
In a bad mood, you might see only the dark side of events that are actually neutral.
In a good mood, you might see the bright side of trauma.

The more something means to you, the more you'll remember it.
Give moments meaning to remember them.
Take away meaning to forget.

You remember what's important.
The first time you were burned, you didn't try to remember that fire is hot.
It hurt, so your brain remembered it effortlessly.
When you make a big mistake and want to learn its lesson, deliberately amplify the pain, the deep regret, and the consequences.
Keep the bad feelings vivid and visceral.
Make the lesson memorable, so you won't do it again.

Without memories, you have no sense of self.
You have to remember your past to see your trajectory.
You use your past to make your future.

Making memories is the most important thing you can do with your life.
The more memories you create, the longer and richer your life feels.
Making memories is how to live.

HERE'S HOW TO LIVE:
MASTER SOMETHING.

Be a monomaniac on a mission to be truly great at something difficult.

Pick one thing and spend the rest of your life getting deeper into it.

Mastery is the best goal because the rich can't buy it, the impatient can't rush it, the privileged can't inherit it, and nobody can steal it.
You can only earn it through hard work.
Mastery is the ultimate status.

Striving makes you happy.
Pursuit is the opposite of depression.
People at the end of their life, who said they were the happiest with their life, were the ones who had spent the most time in the flow of fascinating work.

Concentrating all of your life's force on one thing gives you incredible power.
Sunlight won't catch a stick on fire.
But if you use a magnifying glass to focus the sunlight on one spot, it will.
Mastery needs your full focused attention.

The more you learn about something, the more there is to learn.
You see what normal people don't see.
The path gets more and more interesting as you go.

The pursuit of mastery helps you think long-term.
It keeps your eyes on the horizon.
You resist the temptation of what you want now.
You remember the importance of what you want most.
You spend time intentionally.
Every month has a milestone.
Every day has a goal.
The most rewarding things in life take years.
Only bad things happen quickly.

Decisions are easy when you have only one priority.
Your destination is a huge mountain peak on the horizon.
You can see it from everywhere.
Yes to that mountain, and no to everything else.
You'll always know where you're going, and what you're doing next.
All paths go either towards that mountain or away from it.

Because of this perspective, problems won't deter you.
Most people look down at the ground, upset by every obstacle.
With your eyes on the horizon, you'll step over obstacles, undeterred.

If you haven't decided what to master, pick anything that scares you, fascinates you, or infuriates you.
Don't ask, "Is this the real me?" or "Is this my passion?"
Those questions lead to endless searching and disappointment.
People don't fail by choosing the wrong path — they fail by not choosing.
Make your choice, then make a lifetime commitment to constant improvement.
The passion comes after you start getting good.

Define "success" for yourself.
Describe the outcome you want.
You can't hit a target you can't see.

You need to understand something very counter-intuitive about goals.
Goals don't improve your future.
Goals only improve your present actions.
A good goal makes you take action immediately.
A bad goal doesn't.
A goal shows what's right and wrong.
What moves you towards your goal is right.
What doesn't is wrong.

When you first start learning, you improve massively every week.
Beginning is fun.
But real expertise comes only after years of hard work.
The challenge is staying on the path.

You need ritual, not inspiration.
Every day, no matter what, you must practice.
Your practice ritual is your highest priority — an unbreakable commitment.
Stubbornly protect this time against the demands of the world.

Once you get momentum, never stop.
It's easy to continue, but if you stop, it's hard to start again.
Never miss a day.

When you're not practicing, remember: someone somewhere is practicing.
When you meet them, they will win.

During your work time, do nothing but work.
Keep your hands on your work, and your mind will follow.
If you get stuck, just stop and close your eyes.
The vacuum will extract your actions again.

How many push-ups could you do right now?
But how many could you do if you took a ten-minute break between each set?
Many more.
That's the secret.
Take tiny breaks when working, to go longer than most.

Focus means head down.
Big picture means head up.
The more you're doing of one, the less you're doing of the other.
If you've been head-down on a task for too long, lift your head up to make sure you're going the right way.
Don't do well what you shouldn't do at all.

Pursuing mastery is ambitious, which helps your chance of success.
Most people fail in life not by aiming too high, but by aiming too low.
If you aim high and miss, you don't actually fail.

Move to the most ambitious place in your field.
(Actor? Hollywood. Tech? Silicon Valley. Etc.)
Expectations there are so high that they'll help push you to be the best.
You want the pressure.
You want the stress.

Don't live somewhere pleasant surrounded by normal people.
Live among your fellow freaks, where obsession is normal and ambition is rewarded.

You don't get extreme results without extreme actions.
If you do what most people do, you get what most people get.
Don't be normal.
Society's guidelines are for the lost — not for you.

You don't need a spouse or kids.
You don't need to hang out, make small talk, or join in common rituals.
You don't need to sleep at normal hours, keep a tidy home, or even relax.
Be sharply focused, not well-rounded.

Think of the legendary achievers: the geniuses, brilliant artists, record-breaking athletes, or self-made billionaires.
Do you think those people were well-balanced?
Of course not.
They focused all their energy only on one thing.
That's why they were great.
Pursue your mission at the expense of everything else.

Nobody cares what you're bad at, and neither should you.
Amplify your strengths.
Nobody will see the rest.

Keep the rest of your life boring.
Drama is a distraction.
Your personal life can shrink to almost nothing.
Focus everything on your work.

Mastery is not about doing many things.
It's doing one thing insanely well.
The more you take on, the less you'll achieve.
Say no to everything but your mission.
This is your one contribution to the world.

You don't need new ideas.
You need to master the idea you've begun.
That's why you can ignore all distractions.
The world has no information that you need.

Resist the urge to branch out into something new.
You can do anything, but not everything.

Remember the saying "jack of all trades, master of none".
That's the opposite of you.
You are master of one.

Your focus will almost certainly lead to success.
When you live, dream, and work with one single mission, you
will achieve that mission.
But beware of money and fame.
Money can pull you towards your mountain, but sometimes it
pulls you away.
Fame tries to pull you out of the deep path of mastery into the
shallow gutter of flattery.
The best response to fame's endless requests is a simple
mantra: "No. No. No. No. No."

How long will it take you to become a master?
It doesn't matter.
Imagine getting to a mountaintop after a long hike through a
gorgeous forest.
Achieving your goal would feel like taking off your backpack.
That's all.
You do it for the journey, not the destination.

Pursuing mastery is how to live.

HERE'S HOW TO LIVE:
LET RANDOMNESS RULE.

We think we see patterns and causes.
Really there are none.
We think events are meaningful.
Really they're just coincidence.
We're not used to the logic of probability.
Life is more random than it seems.

Identical twins were separated at birth and raised on opposite
sides of the world.
They met later in life, and found that they had freakishly
identical preferences and circumstances.
What you think is free will might actually be your DNA.
Where you go, what you do, and what you want are accurately
predicted by algorithms.
You are less random than you seem.

So randomize your life.
Use a random generator — an app, a roll of the dice, or a
shuffled deck of cards — to make all of your life's decisions.
Choose a life where you choose nothing.
Let the random generator decide what you do, where you go,
and who you meet.

It'll scramble your habits.
It'll break the myth of causality.
It'll guide you to see places you'd never ordinarily see, and do
what you never would have done.

Randomness keeps your mind open and observant.
You can't predict, so you see clearly.
You can't use old solutions and rules-of-thumb.
You can't blame karma, astrology, demons, saints, anyone or
anything else.

You can't think there's a master plan.

Instead, you'll calculate probability.
You'll be hyper-aware that statistics apply to all of us, and
we're more average than we think.
Life is determined not by causes, but by randomness and odds.
By taking a minute to do the math, you'll have a clearer
understanding of why things are the way they are.

Let your random generator choose what you wear and how you
cut your hair.
Let it send you to events you ordinarily wouldn't have
attended, including classes to learn skills you ordinarily
wouldn't have learned.
You'll become a member of groups you never would have
chosen.
Eventually, you'll look, act, and socialize very differently than
your previous self.
You won't define yourself by these things anymore, since you
didn't choose them.

When talking with people, ask deep open-ended questions
— like "What's your biggest regret?" — that will lead to
unexpected stories.
When ordering in a restaurant, ask them to surprise you.
When doing creative work, let the random generator make
your artistic decisions, shaking up your usual style.

Let your random generator decide where you live every year.
That increases the randomness of everything else.

Ask anyone "Why?" on any subject, and they'll make up
explanations.
They think everything has a reason, and won't believe it's
random.
You'll know everything is random, and won't believe it has a
reason.

Randomness helps you learn acceptance.
You can't take the blame for failures.
You can't take credit for successes.
You can't regret what you didn't cause.

How liberating to not decide and not predict anything.
Stoics and Buddhists work hard to feel indifferent to outcomes.
But you'll feel detachment as a natural side effect of every day being random.
Since nothing has consequences, you'll greet everything with healthy indifference.
Neither upset nor joy — just seeing it as it is.
Thanks to randomness, you'll know that none of it has meaning.

You'll be living a lesson that everyone should learn.
Random stuff happens.
All you can control is your response.
Every day, you'll practice how to react to chaos: with dignity, poise, and grace.

Here's how to live: Pursue pain.

Everything good comes from some kind of pain.
Muscle fatigue makes you healthy and strong.
The pain of practice leads to mastery.
Difficult conversations save your relationships.

But if you avoid pain, you avoid improvement.
Avoid embarrassment, and you avoid success.
Avoid risk, and you avoid reward.

Anyone can be their best when things are going well.
But when things go wrong, you see who they really are.
Remember the classic story arc of the hero's journey.
The crisis — the most painful moment — defines the hero.

Improvement is transformation.
It brings the pain of loss of the comfortable previous self.
It brings the pain of a new set of problems.
Wealth brings the pain of responsibility.
Fame brings the pain of expectations.
Love brings the pain of attachment.
If you avoid pain, you avoid what you really want.

The goal of life is not comfort.
Pursuing comfort is both pathetic and bad for you.
Comfort makes you weak and unprepared.
If you overprotect yourself from pain, then every little
challenge will feel unbearably difficult.

People say they're not doing the work because it's hard.
But it's hard because they're not doing the work.

Comfort is a silent killer.
Comfort is quicksand.
The softer the chair, the harder it is to get out of it.

The right thing to do is never comfortable.
How you face pain determines who you are.

Therefore, the way to live is to steer towards the pain.
Use it as your compass.
Always take the harder option.
Always push into discomfort.
Ignore your instincts.

Pain's power relies on surprise.
If you expect it, it's weaker.
If you choose it, it's gone.

Choosing pain makes it bearable.
It loses its power to hurt you.
You become its master, not victim.

Pain is coming anyway.
Don't get a shield.
Get a saddle.
Tame it.

Don't wish for good luck.
Good luck makes you complacent.
Practice thriving with bad luck.
Bad luck makes you resourceful and strong.
No matter what the world throws your way, you can
stand worse.

Choosing pain means pushing past your instincts.
Food that tastes good is bad for you, and vice-versa.
So don't use your feelings as a guide.

Choose pain in small doses to build your resistance to it.

A daily ritual of hard exercise gives a great perspective on
life's other pains.

Put yourself into stressful situations.
Eventually, almost nothing will seem stressful.

Socially, try to get rejected.
Learn about "rejection therapy".
Make audacious requests that you think will be denied.
This removes the pain of rejection.
And you'll be surprised how often they say yes.

The best way to learn a foreign language is to stop speaking
your mother tongue.
No matter how embarrassing or frustrating, communicate
only in your new language.
Necessity is the best teacher.
But it hurts.

Practice taking on the various kinds of pain.
Attempt something that seems impossible — something
that terrifies you.
Give a speech.
Do a ten-day silent meditation.
Quit a habit.
Apologize to someone you wronged.

Don't congratulate yourself if your attempt avoids failure.
Remember: you want the pain.
The sooner you pay a price, the less it costs.

Be absolutely honest with everyone.
Stop lying, completely.
You lie when you're afraid.
You lie to avoid consequences.
Always say the truth.
Take the painful consequences.

You weren't meant to be idle.
You weren't built for sitting and staring at screens.
You live to push, pull, climb, and grow.

The most exhilarating experiences in your life so far were daring.
Your proudest moments were overcoming a struggle.
The best happiness comes after some pain.

The best waves on the beach can knock you over.
That's the best kind of play.

Since you can't avoid problems, just find good problems.
Happiness isn't everlasting tranquility.
Happiness is solving good problems.

That's why we play games.
Games are challenges.
Any challenge can be turned into a game.

The English word "passion" comes from the Latin word "pati", meaning "to suffer or endure".
To be passionate about something is to be willing to suffer for it — to endure the pain it'll bring.

But don't be a masochist.
Be a scholar of pain.
Every pain has a lesson inside, and a reason why it hurts.
Analyze it.
Understand it.

Ghosts don't leave until you've understood their message.
Problems persist until you claim them and solve them.
Face them directly and they'll disappear.

First we figured out how to fly, then how to get to the moon.
After you conquer the little problems, you'll face the better ones.

Facing pain helps you relate to others.
Your problems are never unique.
Whatever problems you've had, many other people have
had the same problem.
We empathize with someone who's struggling.
It opens our hearts more than seeing someone win.

Most people don't get to choose how they suffer.
Once you tame pain for yourself, tame it for others.

The easy road leads to a hard future.
The hard road leads to an easy future.
Steering towards the pain is how to live.

HERE'S HOW TO LIVE:
DO WHATEVER YOU WANT NOW.

The past?
That's what we call our memories.
The future?
That's what we call our imagination.
Neither exists outside of your mind.
The only real time is this moment.
So live accordingly.
Whatever benefits you right now is the right choice.

You know immediately whether you like something or not.
But if someone asks why, you start making up reasons.
The truth is you like it or you don't.
That's it.
That's life.
Do whatever you like.
You don't need explanations.

When people ask the meaning of life, they're looking for
a story.
But there is no story.
Life is a billion little moments.
They're not a part of anything.

People think they'll do something later.
They think they'll have more time in the future than they
do today, as if later is a magical time when everything will
happen.
Forget the whole notion of the future.
There is only today.
If you want to do something, do it now.
If you don't want to do it now, then you don't want to do it
at all, so let it go.

Doing whatever makes you happy now is smart.
When you're happy, you think better.
More of your brain is engaged.
You're more open to possibilities and connecting ideas.
You learn better and are more creative.
So forget the future and past.
Focus fully on whatever fascinates you now.

You don't need a schedule.
Just pay attention to what excites you.
If you're not excited about what you're doing, move on
to something else.

You don't need plans.
Plans are just predictions about what you might want
in the future.
But your future self shouldn't be bound to what your
past self predicted.
So never make plans.
When someone asks, just say you can't know until that day.
All you know is now.

Live like a frog sitting on a lily-pad.
When it feels like it, it jumps to a different one, and stays
until it feels like jumping again.

Your feelings are wise.
Bad feelings mean you need to take action.
Good feelings mean you took the right action.
Following your feelings is the most natural and rewarding
thing to do.

Most problems are not about the real present moment.
They're anxiety, worried that something bad might happen
in the future.
They're trauma, remembering something bad in the past.
But none of them are real.

If you stop and look around the room, and ask yourself if you have any actual problems right now, the answer is probably no. Unless you're in physical pain or danger, the problems were all in your head.
Memories and imagined futures are not real.
The present moment is real and safe.

People with severe amnesia are surprisingly happy.
They can't remember the past, and they don't try to predict the future since they have no trajectory.
They have only the present moment, so they enjoy it without burden.
Follow their example.
Forget the past and future.

Happiness is something to do, someone to love, and something to desire.
Heaven is not what's at the end of the path.
Heaven is the path itself.

Doing whatever you want, at every moment, is how to live.

Here's how to live:
Be a famous pioneer.

Nobody had ever run a mile in under four minutes.
It seemed impossible.
But one day, Roger Bannister did it, and the news spread worldwide.
Over the next two years, thirty-seven people also did it.

This is the power of the pioneer:
To enable the impossible.
To open a new world of possibility.
To show others that they can do it too, and take it even further.
Explorers used to find unknown lands and bring back stories of unfamiliar cultures, which encouraged others to go exploring.
The old finish line becomes the new starting line.

Debussy, Charlie Parker, Jimi Hendrix, and Rakim pioneered new approaches to music.
Rosa Parks, Harvey Milk, Sally Ride, and Malala Yousafzai broke the glass ceiling, encouraging others to rise.
Modern explorers like Tim Ferriss, Neil Strauss, and A.J. Jacobs, instead of finding unknown lands, are finding unknown lifestyles.
Each of them shows new possibilities for the rest of us.

These pioneers were valuable because they got famous.
If someone else innovated in obscurity, they didn't make an impact.
Marco Polo wasn't the first European to reach China, but he was the first to write a book about it. Then his book inspired Christopher Columbus, and so on.

Millions of young adults today are living a life their grandparents didn't know was possible.
They have more options, thanks to the brave adventures of a few people who broke through boundaries.
Pioneers have a massive impact on the world because their stories help people do things they wouldn't have dreamed of otherwise.

A famous pioneer does more for human progress than a billion others who live a normal life.

So if you want to help humanity while having the most exciting life, then the way to live is to be a famous pioneer.
Go to new extremes.
Try new ideas.
Visit undiscovered cultures.
Show what can be done.

Your job is not just to act, but to tell a fascinating story of how you did so, and inspire others to do it.
Make great adventures, but tell greater stories.
Pursue massive media attention, not for vanity or ego, but so your stories can open minds, spark imaginations, and lead to further explorations.

Here's the best way to do it:

First, make a stage name.
Create a company with the same name, and have it own all the rights to everything you do.
Never reveal your real name.
This is to manage the trappings of your upcoming fame.

Find a writer and a publicist to create your first pioneering adventure.
Collaborate with the writer to make a great story arc before you begin.

So, for example, it's not just a story of how you escaped a cult, but how you joined the cult, uncovered a surprising history, fell in love, were almost discovered and captured, then escaped by changing the mind of your captor, and finally learned some interesting counter-intuitive lessons along the way.
Consult with the publicist to make sure it's interesting to the media.
Then begin.

Record everything on video.
Find ways to make the story arc happen in real life.
When you're done, have your writer make it a fascinating story of various lengths for various outlets — making it a great article, book, video, screenplay, stage talk, and more.
Have the publicist get it everywhere — on every popular platform of the day.
Hire a business manager to turn the attention into profit.
Keep half of your profits in the business, and put half into your private savings.
While your team is promoting your last adventure, you and your writer prepare the next one.
Once fame hits, your biggest challenge is to keep creating — to keep momentum.

Repeat this process as long as you'd like.
Your fame will open new doors, making it possible to do even more incredible things.

So how does it end?
One of two ways:

If this life is really your destiny, do it until it kills you.
Always pushing to see how far you can go, if you die during an adventure, you'll die happy, knowing you pushed it as far as you could.

But if you start feeling you've had enough, then write the
ending.
Build the death of your public persona into your last story.
Since you're famous, this will take some planning.
This is why you used a stage name and company from the
start.

Secretly buy a house under your real name in a mundane place
nobody would expect you to be.
Buy some second-hand clothes and practice changing your
appearance and voice.
Make sure your company is in good hands, run by a team you
trust.

Then, when the filming of your final story is done, rent a boat
and disappear near the ocean, letting everyone think you died.
Escape anonymously into your new life.
Since your private company owns the rights, it can license your
stories, shows, books, and more for years to come, funding
your anonymous life.
A benefit of fame is that it carries on without you.

As you watch the world in the following decades, be glad
if many people surpass you and belittle your pioneering
adventures.
Your final act of generosity is your absence.
It leaves a void for others to step into.

HERE'S HOW TO LIVE:
CHASE THE FUTURE.

Live in the world of tomorrow.
Surround yourself only with what's brand new and upcoming.
That's where life is made.
It's the most optimistic environment, full of hope and promises.

It's the smartest way to live.
You're moving forward in time, so you should watch where you're headed.
Go where things are going.

It's the most exciting way to live.
Every day will be like a child's birthday, with surprising new breakthroughs.
It keeps your brain healthy, young, and active.
Since everything will always be new, you won't rely on assumptions or habits.
You'll pay full attention and keep learning every day.

Move to South Korea, and keep an apartment in Songdo, Incheon.
South Korean culture places the highest value on what's new.

Work as a futurist and technology journalist.
Stay on the cutting edge of things so new they barely exist.
Every new invention will come to you first, before the world has heard of it.
Learn the basics of every field, so you can understand new innovations in logistics or chemistry or anything else.

Listen only to new music.
Watch only new shows.
Use only the newest media.

Give away everything you haven't used in a week.
Ownership binds you to the past.
Don't get invested in any one thing.
Stay immersed only in what's coming next.

Spend your social time meeting new people.
You're not the same person you were last year or even last week.
Old friends and family see you as you used to be, and unintentionally discourage your growth.

Replace your personal daily routines.
When something becomes a habit, quit.

Every month, visit China.
Everything there changes so fast that if you miss more than a month, you'll be out of touch.
Every year, visit Singapore, Jakarta, Addis Ababa, Lagos, Mumbai, Ho Chi Minh City, and Silicon Valley.
Each is creating the future in very different ways.

When a new country declares independence, go immediately.
All conversations there will be focused on the future.

Avoid Europe and anywhere that lives in the past.
Places that resist change have no vision, only memories.
Yesterday is gone for good.
The past is dead.
Resurrecting it makes ghosts and zombies.

Avoid religion because faith is not meant to be questioned.
Tradition is the opposite of what you want.
Nothing worshipped will change.

Oppose convention because that's how things were.
Slavery was a convention.
Human sacrifice was a convention.
Denying human rights to women was a convention.

Some day our current conventions will seem as wrong as these. Since you live in the future, start condemning them now.

The best benefit of living this way is how you cut all ties and never look back.
Every day will be like amnesia.
Whatever traumatic thing might have happened in your past, it no longer defines you.
In your world, the past has no power at all.

Chasing the future is how to live.

HERE'S HOW TO LIVE:
VALUE ONLY WHAT HAS ENDURED.

The longer something lasts, the longer it will probably last.
Something that's been around for a year will probably be
around for another year.
Something that's been around for fifty years will probably be
around for another fifty years.

Only the strong survive, so what's still here after decades is
proven to be well-made and well-loved.
The longer something lasts, the more people know and depend
on it, solidifying its place in our world.
Only these proven things are worth your time and attention.

Think back to ten years ago.
Remember the technologies that the media were hyping as the
future?
How many lasted?
It's hard to remember because we haven't heard of most of
them since then.
They didn't stand the test of time.

Old technologies aren't exciting because they aren't changing
as fast.
But they're more important.
Cryptocurrency versus water filtration.
Virtual reality versus air conditioning.
Which gets more media attention?
Which is more important?

The media focuses on what's new, because that's what pays.
Their attention makes new things seem important.
But only time will tell.

New things have some benefits but deeper downsides like
addiction, pollution, scattered focus, or wasted time.
The marketing shouts the benefits and hides the harm.
But the benefits rarely outweigh the downsides.
Only time will tell.

The pleasure of buying a new thing disappears in days,
even hours.
So much misery comes from indulgences in current junk.

So the way to live is to ignore everything new.
All of it.
Let the test of time filter everything.
Value only what has endured.

Ignore all marketing and advertising.
Nobody is pushing what really matters.
Friendships, nature, family, learning, community.
The best things in life aren't things.

Ignore all news.
If it's important, there will eventually be a good book about it.
When people ask you about current news, proudly have no
opinion.
Admit you've given it no thought at all — and don't plan to —
because it's not important.
Indulging is common.
Refraining is rare.

The world of news is noisy, because they have to hype it.
They try to get you to pay attention to something that's not
actually important.
They create a false sense of urgency, social status, fear, shock,

or any tricks possible to manipulate your psychological triggers, and ultimately help them profit.
By contrast, the truly important things are quiet.
Life is incredibly peaceful when you shut out the noise.

The modern life is shallow and distracted.
The timeless life is deep and focused.

Live in the past.
Watch the greatest movies of all time.
Read the classics.
Listen to the legends.
These things have lasted because they work so well.
Time is the best filter.

What technologies have the best future?
The ones with the best past.
Be the last to adopt a technology, after it's cheaper, better, and no longer changing.
Pity the early adopters, exploring the pitfalls, like the first mouse caught in the mousetrap.
Technology advances faster than wisdom.
It's smarter to move at wisdom's pace.
Don't buy a bandage unless you have a wound.

When you need a coat, table, or house, find one old and used.
They're incredibly well-crafted — sturdier and more beautiful than anything new.
They'll outlive you.

Before trying to improve something old, find out why it is the way it is.
Never assume people in the past were ignorant.
They did it that way for good reasons.
Study the past — understand Chesterton's fence — before thinking you know better.

Study history, tradition, and culture.
Get to know places that haven't been homogenized by
globalization.
When a person loses their memory, they lose their sanity.
When a culture loses its traditions, it loses its sanity too.
The world is acting crazy because it doesn't know who it is
anymore.

Move to a small self-sufficient town that has resisted
modernization — ideally an untouched place that hasn't
changed in a hundred years, and won't change in a
hundred more.
Spend time outside.
Find happiness and perspective in nature.
It reminds you that you don't need anything the modern
world is pushing.
Everything they're shouting about will soon be gone.

Learn time-tested skills that were just as useful in your
grandparents' time as they are today.
Speaking, writing, gardening, accounting, persuasion, and
survival skills.
These skills have hardly changed in a century.
They're unlikely to change in your lifetime.

Master the fundamentals, not new tricks.
Learn the timeless aspects of your craft.
This knowledge will never lose its value.
In any given field, learn the oldest thing still around, since
it's the one most likely to last.

Become a geologist.
You'll measure things in millions of years.
Your timeline will be so long that mountains seem fluid.
The whole modern world will seem like a sandcastle, built
and washed away in a single day.

And so, by ignoring the new, you will improve your life
in every way.
Better investment of your time.
Better peace of mind.
Better quality items and entertainment.
Better skill set.
Better perspective.
Better everything.

The best way to live is to value only what has endured.

Here's how to live: Learn.

Learning is underrated.
People wonder why they're not living their ideal life.
Maybe they never learned how.

You get healthy by learning healthy habits.
You get wealthy by learning valuable skills.
You build a great interpersonal life by learning people skills.
Most misery comes from not learning these things.

The biggest obstacle to learning is assuming you already know.
Confidence is usually ignorance.

Never consider yourself an expert.
It's the strong swimmers who drown.

Don't believe what you think.
Have questions, not answers.
Doubt everything.
The easiest person to fool is yourself.

Don't answer a hard question too quickly.
Don't stop at the first answer.
In mystery stories, the first suspect is not the culprit.

If you're not embarrassed by what you thought last year, you
need to learn more and faster.
When you're really learning, you'll feel stupid and vulnerable
— like a hermit crab between shells.

Be surprised by something every day.
Find that exciting moment when you get a new perspective.
Like a movie that reveals something at the end which changes
the way you think of everything you've seen before.
If you're not having these moments often, find new inputs.

Whatever scares you, go do it.
Then it won't scare you anymore.

Whatever you hate, get to know it.
Then you won't hate it anymore.

Talk with people you usually avoid.
Pursue subjects you know nothing about, and experiences
unlike anything you've done before.
If you're not surprised — if you didn't feel your brain
changing — then you didn't really learn.

Don't be consistent with your past self.
Only idiots never change their mind.

Sacrifice the things you used to believe, and the ways you
used to be.
Learning leaves a trail of little deaths.

Remember what you learn.
Know why you're learning.
Information doesn't stick without emotion.
You learn better when you're having fun.

Take notes.
Review them often.
Make flash cards to remind your future self what you
learned today.
Quiz yourself with spaced repetition.
Knowledge fades and eventually disappears unless you
keep it refreshed.

Internalize it.
Don't expect to just look it up when you need it.
Integrate it into how you think.

Get out of your room and try out a new skill in the real world. Go to the physical place where it's happening, and put your ass on the line with something to lose.
A vivid, visceral feeling of danger will teach you better than words.

Knowledge is often described simply — "in a nutshell".
But the inside of a nutshell is complex.
So crack open nutshells to understand them better.
Put concepts in a nutshell to keep them in your pocket and pass them around.

Communicate knowledge to others to make sure you understand.
Don't quote.
Put it in your own words without looking up or referencing what others said.
If you can't explain it yourself, you don't know it.

To communicate clearly, you have to think clearly.
Writing is refined thinking.
Public speaking tests your writing on a real audience.
Great public speaking comes from great private thinking.

Teaching and learning are telepathy.
We can connect across oceans and centuries.
Words written by someone long ago and far away can penetrate your mind.
Share what you learn so it can be received by others, even when you are long gone.

Learning makes you a better person and makes the world a better place.
Learning is a pursuit you can't lose.
As you age, you'll lose muscle and beauty, but you won't lose your wisdom.
Learning is how to live.

HERE'S HOW TO LIVE:
FOLLOW THE GREAT BOOK.

You know what your great book is.
Whether the Bible, Tanakh, Upanishads, Quran, Think and
Grow Rich, Seven Habits of Highly Effective People,
or another, follow it diligently.

Your book is wiser than you.
It's describing natural law — the way our world works.
It's not just someone's opinion.
It has the definitive answers to the choices you're confronted
with each day.
Don't think you know better.

People say they want to make their own decisions.
But imagine that you have a life-or-death medical situation,
so you rush to the doctor, and the doctor says, "There are
hundreds of different approaches we could take. You decide.
It's up to you."
You would say, "No! You're the doctor. You're the expert.
You know best. You decide. Tell me what to do."
Your book is the expert on how to live.
It's helped millions of people.
Defer to its wisdom.

Your book was meant for people exactly like you.
You're not an exception to humanity.
Its rules apply to you.
It guides you on a good life.

If your book is ancient, you may think it's not enough since
it doesn't mention modern life.
But nothing is truly new.
Morals seem like they've changed in recent history.
But really, morals haven't changed in longer history.

If you update the language and some references, books written thousands of years ago sound like they could have been written today.
The human condition remains the same.
Your book has all the wisdom you need.
Read metaphorically, and apply it to your modern life.

You don't lack direction.
You have too many directions.
An open mind, like an open mouth, needs to eventually close on something.
Stop swerving and chasing new leaders.
Stay on a single steady path.
Following your book is how to live.

First, make a "born again" split.
Let go of your old identity.
Let your new self be incongruent with your old self.
Let your friends and family know that you've changed.

Bring your book with you everywhere as a constant reminder and reference.
Refer to its rules in every situation, every day.
Memorize its crucial sentences.
Keep them at the forefront of your mind.

Following rules is smart.
It's efficient.
You don't need to stop and re-think every situation.

"Follow your passion" is terrible advice.
Fleeting interests are a bad compass.
Passions pass so quickly that to follow them would have you dashing around like a dog chasing bubbles.

Don't follow your heart.
Your heart has been hacked.

Your intuition is usually wrong because it's just emotion,
subliminally influenced by amoral inputs.
Emotions are a wild animal.
You need rules to tame them.

Rules give you freedom from your desires.
When you rise above your instincts, you still feel them but
no longer do what they say.
Following your emotions is not freedom.
Being free from following emotions is freedom.

When you stop following emotions, and just do what's right,
then you'll finally get what you always wanted.
It was the emotions that were distracting you all along.

So what's the right thing to do?
An action with good results?
An action that feels good?
No.
The action prescribed by your book.
No need to judge or decide.
Just follow the rules and trust the path.

Rules must be absolutely unbreakable.
If you try to decide, each time, whether it's OK to break the
rule or not, then you've missed the whole point of rules.
Rules are to save you from deciding.
That's why hard rules are easier to keep.

Discipline turns intentions into action.
Discipline means no procrastination.
Discipline means now.
Choose the pain of discipline, not the pain of regret.

An undisciplined moment seems harmless, but they add up
to disaster.
Without discipline, the tiny things will be your downfall.

Self-control is always rewarding.
Self-control is always the right thing to do.
This is a universal law.
Your self-control is highest in the morning and diminishes
during the day, so review your book's rules every afternoon.

Physical discipline helps mental discipline.
Align your outer self with your inner self.
Cleaning your house helps clean your mind.

Discipline gets you to your destination.
Without it, you're led astray by everyone else.
If you don't obey your constraints, persuasive people and
technology will pull you their way.

People beg you to bend your rules to fit their agenda.
So blame your book when you refuse.
Saying "the book says so" helps your burden of responsibility.
If someone challenges your choices or asks you to explain, just
say "the book says so" and carry on without the exhausting
debate.

Some people may surpass you by breaking the rules.
But remember: the miserable, broken, destitute people in the
world are the other outcome of breaking the rules.
Many more fail than succeed.
Rules may keep you from some stupendous heights, but they
will always keep you from falling too low.

Define a good life as more than shallow pleasure.
A good life is contribution.
A good life is resisting temptation.
A good life is being the best you can be.
A good life is diligently following your book.

Here's how to live: Laugh at life.

A gorilla, speaking with sign language, makes a joke.
We're amazed.
She's showing the fullest expression of a soul.

But when a person is humorless, it's the opposite.
They've lost the point of life.

A recovering hospital patient makes a joke.
We're relieved.
Not just their body, but their soul is alive.

But when a previously jovial patient loses their humor, we're rightfully concerned.
They're losing the spark of life.

What does this tell us?

Humor is the spirit of life — a sign of a healthy, vibrant mind and soul.

Humor means using your mind beyond necessity, beyond reality, for both noticing and imagining.
That's why we admire a quick wit.
It shows you quickly looked at something from many angles, found the one that amused you the most, and considerately expressed it to someone else.
Observation, creativity, and empathy, all in an instant.
What could be a better sign of a healthy mind?

Think of any action movie where the hero thinks he's got the villain trapped, but then the villain starts laughing.
Laughing?
What does he know that we don't?
What unseen advantage would make him laugh when he seems to be at an end?

To laugh at something is to be superior to it.
Humor shows internal control.

Think of the comic heroes, like Charlie Chaplin, Jackie Chan, Jim Carrey, Kung Fu Panda, or Roberto Benigni in "Life Is Beautiful".
They win by being playful, creative, adaptive, irreverent, and unbound by norms.
Those who take life too seriously are the opposite, and at a disadvantage.

No matter what you need to do, there's a playful, creative way to do it.
Playing gives you personal autonomy and power.
When kids play make-believe, anything goes.
To play is to be free from constraints.

You can make light of anything.
Respond to life's events however you want.
Nothing has to get you down.

A bad situation can feel all-consuming.
A laugh shows you've escaped.
Humor puts distance between an event and yourself.
Comedy is tragedy plus time.
Time belittles anything by showing it's not as bad as it seemed.
Humor does that instantly.

Someone says life is hard.
The comedian says, "Compared to what?"
Comedians are philosophers.

Humor helps you see the familiar from a surprising new perspective.
It reminds you that there is no grand truth.
Any belief can be up-ended.

Every belief can be mocked.
Nobody knows anything.
See?
Laughing is subversive.

Comedy doesn't care what's true, and neither should you.
Whatever makes you happy is what works.
Humor transcends reason.

Life is meaningless.
That's what's funny.

Besides, it makes you very appealing.
Everyone wants to be with someone who's having more fun.

At every moment in life, choose whatever action or angle
amuses you.
Laughing at life is how to live.

HERE'S HOW TO LIVE:
PREPARE FOR THE WORST.

Things are going to get harder.
The future will test your strength.

So far, you've lived in a time of prosperity.
You haven't experienced massive devastation, but you
probably will.
It'll be harder to make money.
It'll be harder to be happy.
Much of what you love now will be gone.
You'll look back at this year as one of the easiest you ever had.

You'll get injured or sick, losing some of your ability to see,
hear, move, or think.
You'll wish for the health you have now.

How can you thrive in an unknowable future?
Prepare for the worst.
Train your mind to be ready for whatever may come.
This is how to live.

The future is unpredictable and uncontrollable.
Picture all the things that could go wrong.
Prepare for each, so they won't surprise or hurt you.

Never worry.
This isn't emotional.
Just anticipate and prepare.

Remember the fable of the ant and the grasshopper?
The grasshopper was just enjoying the summer, teasing the ant
for working instead of relaxing.
Then winter came, and the grasshopper starved, but the ant
was ready.

Disasters come suddenly, without warning.
Tragedy hurts the most when it's unexpected.
But if you expect it, you take away its power.

Do you know what's behind each mountain of a challenge?
More mountains.

Expecting life to be wonderful is disappointing.
Expecting life to be disappointing is wonderful.
If you expect to be disappointed, you won't be.

Vividly imagine the worst scenarios until they feel real.
Accepting them is the ultimate happiness and security.
Realize that the worst is not that bad.

People talk about pessimism and optimism by saying, "Glass
half-empty or glass half-full?"
But a caveman would say, "Oh my god! A glass! What a great
invention! I can see what I'm about to drink! This is amazing!
A blanket! A chair! A bed! Food, ready and waiting? This is
heaven!"
You don't have to be a caveman to look around you and
appreciate your comforts by imagining life without them.
Then imagine the relief of finding shelter, the joy of controlled
fire on command, and the satisfaction of hot water.

To appreciate something fully, picture losing it.
Imagine losing your freedom, reputation, money, and home.
Imagine losing your ability to see, hear, walk, or talk.
Imagine the people you love dying tomorrow.
Never take them for granted.

Luxury is the enemy of happiness because you adapt to its
comforts.
Luxury makes you soft, weak, and harder to satisfy.
(Pity people who can't enjoy anything less than the best.)
Never accept luxury, or you'll find it hard to do without

because it will feel like loss.

Comfort reduces your future happiness.
You get upset that your meal doesn't come as ordered, or
angry at your phone for having an imperfect connection.
You lose appreciation.
You forget the perspective of how bad things could be.

Practice being uncomfortable, even in small ways.
Take the stairs instead of the elevator.
Skip eating for a day, or sugar for a month.
Go light-weight camping for a week.
Befriend discomfort so that you'll never fear it.

Your biggest enemy is insatiability.
Recognize your desire to be entertained by life, and break
the habit.
Practice being happy with what you have.

Own as little as possible.
When you realize you're dependent on something, get rid
of it to prove you don't need it.
The less you have, the less you have to lose.

Want nothing, and nothing will disappoint you.
Want nothing, and nothing is outside your control.
Want nothing, and fate can't hurt you.

Distinguish between what's in your control and what isn't.
If it's not in your control, put it out of your head.
Trying to control outcomes makes you disappointed and
resentful.
Focus only on your thoughts and actions.

Your circumstances in life don't actually change your
happiness.
People who become paralyzed or win the lottery go back
to being as happy as they were before.

So don't depend on circumstances.
Everything that happens is neutral.
Your beliefs label it as good or bad.
The only way to change your happiness is to change your beliefs.

Did someone make you angry?
Did a situation make you sad?
No.
It's all you.
Nothing is good or bad.
You just reacted as if it was.
When something bad happens, ask, "What's great about this?"
Instead of changing the world, just change your reactions.

When something happens, don't interpret.
No story, no "should have", no judgment, not even an opinion.
This is seeing clearly.

Your goal is grateful indifference.
Win the lottery?
Go to jail?
Get famous?
Go blind in an accident?
It doesn't matter because you're fine either way.
Detach from the outcome and be OK no matter what happens.

My neighbor has a dog that attacks strangers and has even bitten a child.
When people complain, my neighbor says he can't help it.
"Dogs will be dogs."
Wrong!
Dogs can be tamed.
He just never trained his dog.
Instead he acts like the situation is hopeless, and makes it everyone else's problem.

This is how most people are about their emotions.
They say, "I can't help the way I feel."
Wrong!
Emotions can be tamed.
You are in control.
The problem comes from going easy on yourself.
Instead, train your emotions like you would a dog.

Shallow happy is having a donut.
Deep happy is having a fit body.

Shallow happy is what you want now.
Deep happy is what you want most.

Shallow happy serves the present.
Deep happy serves the future.

Shallow happy is trying to conquer the world.
Deep happy is conquering yourself.

Shallow happy is pursuing pleasure.
Deep happy is pursuing fulfillment.

Fulfillment is more fun than fun.

Visit your favorite places.
Listen to your favorite music.
Taste your favorite food.
Touch your favorite people.
This might be the last time you do all these things, so
appreciate each moment fully.

All of this appreciation is practice for death.
When death comes, you'll treat it with the same indifference
as everything else.
You've been preparing for it all along.

HERE'S HOW TO LIVE: FOR OTHERS.

Focusing on yourself seems smarter and easier, but it's short-sighted.
It's ignoring the huge benefit of cooperation.

Compare survival strategies.
You could prepare for disaster by stocking food and ammunition in a bunker by yourself.
But what if, instead:
You made yourself an integral member of your community.
You built a reputation of being helpful and generous.
And many people around you cared about your well-being.
Obviously, this is a better strategy.

Even if you prefer solitude, you have to admit that being a valuable member of a group is smarter.
The best way to be safe is to help others be safe.
The best way to be connected is to help others be connected.
People look out for each other.
But nobody helps the unhelpful.
You can't actually pull yourself up by your bootstraps.
Ultimately you are lifted by those around you.

Never say, "Not my problem."
We're all in this together.
What's good for your community is good for you.
Whatever affects others affects you.
The quality of your life is tied to the quality of your community, neighborhood, and country.
You can't be healthy in a sick society.

Psychologists, philosophers, and religions all agree
on one thing.
Helping others is a better path to happiness than
helping only yourself.
Giving makes you happier than receiving.
People with strong social ties live longer, healthier,
happier lives.
The most miserable people are self-absorbed.
So aim to be the opposite.

Living for others is how to live.

After age twenty, you need deliberate effort to
make new friends.
Friends are made, not found.
If you sincerely appreciate someone, and really
engage with their interests, you will become friends.

Ask open-ended questions, asking people's thoughts.
Ask them to elaborate on whatever they've said.
Show that you're interested.
Allow silence.
Don't fill it.
Silence gives space to think, and an invitation to
contribute without pressure.

Small talk is just a way of matching the other person's
tone and mood.
It helps them be comfortable with you.

Be warm, open, and fully present with everyone
you encounter.
Confidence attracts.
Vulnerability endears.

Assume everyone is just as smart and deep as you.
Assume their temperament is just their nature, and not
their fault.
Don't be mad at them for being that way, for the same
reason you can't be mad at someone for being tall.

Appreciate differences.
A conversation with a clone of yourself would be boring.

Whenever you're thinking something nice about someone,
tell them.
A sincere compliment can put a lot of fuel in someone's tank.
People don't hear enough compliments.

Be consistent.
People can only depend on you if you're consistent.
Meet up regularly to maintain each friendship, so the
connections grow stronger.
Be patient with your friends, even for years at a time.
Real friendship doesn't end.

Relationships are more delicate than people.
Relationships can be ruined with one inconsiderate word.
Withhold angry thoughts, and let the feeling pass
unexpressed.
Never lose your cool.
Never vent.
Always be kind, no matter how you feel.

Imagine if you found out someone was going to die tomorrow.
Imagine how much attention, compassion, and generosity
you'd give them.
Imagine how you'd forgive their faults.
Imagine what you'd do to make their last day on Earth the
best it could be.
Now treat everyone like that, every day.

Sometimes you really need emotional support.
You're going through a hard time or a big decision.
You need someone else's perspective on your situation.

Friends or family can give wonderful comfort.
You share your problem, and they share the burden.
They care for you deeply, but aren't as distraught, so you see yourself through their eyes, and realize it's not as bad as it feels.

An objective mentor can give this effect even more so.
This person has less sympathy, and a dispassionate perspective.
You summarize the facts of your situation with less indulgence and hyperbole.
Hearing yourself tell this version of your story reduces the intensity of your emotions.
You see yourself as they do: as a smaller character in a bigger picture.

Some people like support groups for this same reason.
Telling your tale to a group of indifferent strangers both shares and dilutes the pain.

Success in business comes from helping people — bringing the most happiness to the most people.
The best marketing is being considerate.
The best sales approach is listening.
Serve your clients' needs, not your own.
Business, when done right, is generous and focused on others.
It draws you out of yourself, and puts you in service of humanity.

The most extreme version of living for others is becoming famous.
Do everything in public, for the public.
Share everything you do, even though it's extra work.
It's giving yourself to the world.
But being famous means you'll never be able to reciprocate enough.

Your caring should grow until it reaches past your community, past your country, past your generation, and past your species.
Care about strangers across the world as much as you do your family.
Care about all forms of life as much as you do humans.

Living for others is how to live.

HERE'S HOW TO LIVE: GET RICH.

Suspend judgment.
Making money isn't evil, greedy, shallow, or vain.
Money isn't your worth as a human being, or a
substitute for love.
But don't pretend it doesn't matter.

Money can represent freedom, safety, experience,
generosity, attractiveness, power, or whatever you want.
But really, money is as neutral as math.
Because it's neutral, people have projected all kinds
of meaning onto it.
Your biggest obstacle to getting rich is the harmful
meaning you've attached to it.
Your biggest advantage can be projecting a helpful
meaning onto it.
Make it mean you're on the right path.
Make it a game.
Make it mean you're free.

Or consider this:
Money is nothing more than a neutral exchange of value.
Making money is proof you're adding value to people's lives.
Aiming to get rich is aiming to be useful to the world.
It's striving to do more for others.
Serving more.
Sharing more.
Contributing more.
The world rewards you for creating value.
Pursue wealth because it's moral, good, and unlimited.

Money is social.

It was invented to transfer value between people.

One job pays way more than another because it has more social value.

To get rich, don't think about what's valuable to you.

Think about what's valuable to others.

To do the opposite is the cliché of the starving artist: creating something that's valuable to you, but not to others.

Money doesn't care about your race, gender, education, physique, family, or nationality.

Anyone can be rich.

Someone always will, so it might as well be you.

Making money is a skill like any other.

Learn it and practice it as you would anything else.

Money is a great motivator.

It works better than force, rules, punishment, or appealing to generosity.

Great art has been created in pursuit of profit.

Numbers reveal truth and opportunity.

With every business idea you have or hear, do the math to run the projections and implications.

Study profitable companies the way an artist studies great art.

Apply their best techniques to your own pursuit.

Doing the math helps you think critically, be realistic, and make better decisions.

The world is full of money.

There's no shortage.

So capture the value you create.

Charge for what you do.

It's unsustainable to create value without asking anything in return.

Remember that many people like to pay.

The more something costs, the more people value it.
By charging more, you're actually helping them use it and appreciate it.
Charge more than is comfortable to your current self-image.
Value yourself higher, then rise to fit this valuation.

Be fully committed to getting rich, or it won't happen.
Adjust your self-image so that you congruently feel that you should and will be rich.
If you subconsciously don't feel you deserve it, you'll sabotage your pursuit.
But if you truly feel you deserve it, you'll do whatever it takes.
So adjust your self-image first.

Don't aim to just be comfortable.
You don't make the world a better place by just getting by.
If you aim to be comfortable, you won't get rich.
But if you aim to be rich, you'll also be comfortable.
Aiming to be rich makes you think bigger, which is more exciting, more fun, and less conventional since most people don't think big.

The world needs more boldness.
Refuse the comfortable addiction of a steady paycheck.
Boldly jump on opportunities.
Take risky action.

Create your own business.
Come up with a brand name that can be attached to any business.
(Perhaps it's your name.)
Use it for the rest of your life on everything of quality.
A recognized brand can charge a premium price, earning more than unrecognized names.
Instead of thinking of customers as leading to a sale, think of each sale as leading to a life-long relationship with a customer.

Use other people's ideas.
Ideas are worth almost nothing.
Execution is everything.
The world is filled with ideas, yet so few take action and
make them happen.
Better to be filled with action than ideas.
Best of all to be the owner.
Own and control 100% of whatever you create.

Boring industries have little competition, since most people
are seeking status in glamorous new fields.
Find an old industry and solve an old problem in a new way.
Your innovation might be behind the scenes, like owning the
entire supply chain.

Avoid difficult business problems.
Your time is more profitably spent doing what comes easily
to you.

Avoid competition.
Never be another contender in the crowd, fighting for scraps.
It doesn't pay to do something anyone can do.
Be separate — in a category of your own.
Invent something completely new.
Instead of fighting to split an existing dollar, inventing
creates a dollar out of thin air.
Invent for a very small niche of people who need something
that doesn't exist.
Instead of making a key, then looking for a lock, find
something locked, then make its key.

Follow the rising tides of where profits are going.
Get in early on an industry that's developing quickly.
More risk, more opportunity, more investors, more rewards.

Once your business is successful, stay paranoid.
Technology is improving faster, so a successful business model
doesn't last as long as it used to.
You'll be disrupted by others if you don't keep improving or
disrupting yourself.

Sell your business before you have to.
Sell before it peaks.
The fun is in creating a business, not maintaining it.

As soon as you have extra money, invest it.

Investing is counter-intuitive.
You need to ignore your gut and heart.
Follow dispassionate reason.
Be disciplined, not clever.
It's a matter of math, not mood.
Emotions are the enemy of investing.

Investing is easy unless you try to beat the market.
Settle for average.
Be happy with a good-enough return from passive index funds
that represent the entire world economy.
Just take a few minutes per year to rebalance.
Don't over-think it.
It's better to do nothing than something.
Keep it simple and manage it yourself.
Avoid exciting investments.

Speculating is not investing.
Never speculate.
Never predict.
Be humble, not arrogant.
Never think for one second that you know the future.
Remind yourself over and over again that nobody knows
the future.
Ignore anyone that says they do.

Money is your servant, not your master.
Don't act rich.
Don't lose touch with regular people.
Stay frugal.
Reducing your expenses is so much easier than increasing your income.

You don't need to tell anyone you have money.
You don't even need to spend it.
Don't buy too many things, too big of a house, or hire too many people.
Rich people who do this feel trapped and miserable.
The less you buy, the more you're in control.
Forget lifestyle.
Forget yourself.
Stay 100% focused on creating value.
Everything else is a corrupting distraction.

Nothing destroys money faster than seeking status.
Don't show off.
Don't invest in a business you don't control.
Don't loan money to a friend, or you'll lose your money and your friend.
You'd be better off just giving them the money.
The return is the same ($0), but you'd skip the bad feelings.

Don't convince yourself your home is an asset.
Your home is an expense, not an investment, because it doesn't put money in your pocket each month.

When you're rich, everything feels free.
A $5000 expense feels like it costs a dollar.
It doesn't dent your bank account.
Money will be like tap water.
It's always there.
You don't need to think about it.

One downside is you don't get excited about money anymore.
It used to feel so exciting to make $5000.
Now you don't even notice it.
Someone could give you another million dollars, and it wouldn't change a thing.
You don't need it, since there's nothing you want to buy.
The extra millions won't make you extra happy.
You'll work harder to keep your money than you will to make more.
As with sex, the fascination fades when you have plenty.

Say no to more stuff.
Say yes to more choices.

Then you'll get philosophical, since you'll have all the options in the world.
You'll find your riches are worthless, and maybe even an obstacle, when it comes to friendship and love.
Money makes problems go away, but amplifies personality traits.
Money won't change you, but it will amplify who you are.

You only need to get rich once.
When you win a game, you stop playing.
Don't be the dragon in the mountain, just sitting on your gold.
Don't lose momentum in life.
Once you've done it, take it with you and do something else.

HERE'S HOW TO LIVE:
REINVENT YOURSELF REGULARLY.

People say everything is connected.
They're wrong.
Everything is disconnected.
There is no line between moments in time.

Something happened.
Something else happened.
People love stories, so they connect two events,
calling them cause and effect.
But the connection is fiction.

It's a hard fiction to escape.
"My parents did that, so that's why I did this."
No.
Those two events are not connected.
There is no line between moments in time.

Same with definitions.
"I'm an introvert, so that's why I can't."
No.
Definitions are not reasons.
Definitions are just your old responses to past situations.
What you call your personality is just a past tendency.
New situations need a new response.

Are you more emotional or intellectual?
Early bird or night owl?
Liberal or conservative?
No.
Disagree with the question.
You aren't supposed to be easy to explain.

Putting a label on a person is like putting a label
on the water in a river.
It's ignoring the flow of time.

Your identity.
Your meanings.
Your trauma.
They're all based on the core idea that you're in a
continuum, living a story.
But there is no line between moments in time.
There is no story.
There is no plot.

Should you try to be consistent with your past self?
Should a newspaper try to be consistent with past news?
You're an ongoing event — a daily improvisation —
responding to the situation of the moment.

Your past is not your future.
Whatever happened before has nothing at all to do with
what happens next.
There is no consistency.
Nothing is congruent.
Never believe a story.

You've changed so much over time.
Your past self is as different from your current self as you are
from other people.
Your past self needs to step down, like a previous president,
to let the new you run the show.

Doing what you've always done is bad for your brain.
If you don't change, you'll age faster and get stuck.

The way to live is to regularly reinvent yourself.

Every year or two, change your job and move somewhere new.
Change the way you eat, look, and talk.
Change your preferences, opinions, and usual responses.
Try the opposite of before.

Disconnect from your past.
Cut all common threads.
Keep nothing permanent.
No tattoos.
Remain a clean slate.

At every little decision, ten times a day, choose the
thing you haven't tried.
Act out of character.
It's liberating.
Get your security not from being an anchor, but from
being able to ride the waves of change.

Let go of your expertise.
You built that boat to cross that river, so leave it there.
Don't drag it along with you.
The timid cling to achievements.
The wise keep their hands free.

Nature changes seasons at regular intervals.
So should you.
We can't prolong one season.
Never stay too long.
Knowing something is going to end gives you
more appreciation for it.

Every reinvention is the beginning,
which is the most exciting time.
Like a promise, just given.

Here's how to live: Love.

Not love, the feeling, but love the active verb.
It's not something that happens to you.
It's something you do.
You choose to love something or someone.
You can love anything or anyone you decide to love.

Love is a combination of attention, appreciation, and empathy.

To love something, first you have to connect with it.
Give it your full attention.
Deliberately appreciate it.
Try this with places, art, and sounds.
Try this with activities and ideas.
Try this with yourself.

Many times a day, you have the opportunity to connect.
You can dash through a place, or stop to appreciate it.
You can do an activity absent-mindedly, or pay full
attention to every detail of it.
(Work is love in action.)
You can make shallow small-talk, or really get to
know someone.
Choose to connect every time.

Sharing is connecting.
Share your knowledge.
Share your home.
Share your time.

Learning is loving.
The more you learn about something, the more you can love it.
Learn about a place to appreciate it.
Learn about people to empathize with them.
Not just individuals, but cultures, mindsets, and worldviews.

If you are apathetic about or against something, learn
more about it.

Actively listen to people.
When they're succinct, ask them to elaborate.
People aren't used to someone being sincerely interested,
so they'll need some coaxing to continue.
But never try to fix them.
When someone tells you what's broken, they want you to
love the brokenness, not try to eliminate it.

Break down the walls that separate you from others and
prevent real connections.
Take off your sunglasses.
Don't text when you should talk.
Avoid habitual comebacks and clichés.
Admit what you're really feeling, even when it's
uncomfortable.
Keep communicating instead of shutting down.
We think walls protect us from enemies, but walls are what
create enemies in the first place.

The hardest part of connecting with someone is being honest.
If you say what you think someone wants to hear, you're
preventing a real connection.
Manners are shallow.
Honesty is deep.
Always tell the real truth, or they'll never know the real you,
so you'll never really feel loved.

Honesty is an ideal that's always a little further away.
It has no finish line.
No matter how honest you are, there's always more honest.

Don't exaggerate to be more entertaining.
Don't downplay.
If you downplay your achievements to make someone else

comfortable, you're preventing connection with that person and even with yourself.
Just be honest.
If you've done something great, say so.
If you're not doing well, say so.

If you have feelings for someone, and you don't let that person know, you're lying with your silence.
Be direct.
It saves so much trouble and regret.

You could live with others, pleasing only them.
You could live in solitude, pleasing only yourself.
But ideally, when with others, be the same person you'd be when alone.

The more you really connect with people, the more you learn about yourself: what excites you, what drains you, what attracts you, and what intimidates you.

And then there's romantic love.
You never really regret falling in love.
Do it as much as possible.

Flirting and romance is like eating dessert first.
After you come down from the sugar rush, you get to the more nourishing part of the meal.

Beware of the feeling that someone completes you or will save you.
You have wounds in your past.
You have needs that were ignored.
You seek someone to fill these gaps — someone that has traits you crave.
But nobody will save you.
You have to fill those gaps yourself.
When you're going through an unstable time in your life,

you latch on to whatever makes you feel stable.
Instant obsessive love is a bad sign that you're thinking of
someone as the solution.
Projecting perfection onto someone is not love.
You say "I love you" but really mean "I love this".

Notice how you feel around people.
Notice who brings out the best in you.
Notice who makes you feel more connected with yourself —
more open and more honest.
Don't worry about anyone's opinion of you.
Don't hope that someone is impressed.
Impress yourself.
Be your ideal self.
If that's not impressive, then nothing would be.
If the relationship isn't going to work, it's better to know early,
instead of hiding your true self and putting up a façade for a
long time before finding out.

Between any two people is a third thing: the relationship itself.
Actively nurture it.
If you improve it, it will improve you.

Once you're in a relationship, avoid harming it.
It's easy to love someone's best qualities, but it's work
to love their flaws.
Don't try to change someone, or teach them a lesson,
unless they ask you to.

When one of you is being childish, the other needs to
be the adult.
Like a dance, you can't both dip at the same time.
One of you has to stay upright to keep the other from
collapsing.

Unless you are drops of liquid, one plus one never equals one.
You must both be free and able to live without each other.

Be together by choice, not necessity or dependence.
Love your partner, but don't need your partner.
Need is insatiable.
Need destroys love.

If you choose not to love someone, break up with one last
boost of love, empathy, and kindness, instead of showing
your lack of love.

Be wary of marriage.
Don't make a life-long commitment based on an emotional
state.
It's illegal to sign contracts when drunk, so you shouldn't
sign a marriage contract when drunk on infatuation.

Having a child is like being in love.
It's such a tight bond.
You're so close.
So much trust.
So much support.
But, just like the other people you love, your child's interests
and values will be different than yours.

You don't love someone to shape their future.
You don't judge your friendships by how successful your
friend becomes.
So don't love and judge your children that way.
Don't try to change them.
Just give them a great environment where they can thrive.
Give them safety to experiment, make mistakes, and fail up.

The saddest life is one without love.
The happiest life is filled with love.
Choose to love as much as you can.
Loving is how to live.

HERE'S HOW TO LIVE: CREATE.

The most valuable real estate in the world is the graveyard.
There lie millions of half-written books, ideas never launched,
and talents never developed.
Most people die with everything still inside of them.

The way to live is to create.
Die empty.
Get every idea out of your head and into reality.

Calling yourself creative doesn't make it true.
All that matters is what you've launched.
Make finishing your top priority.

When most people see modern art, they think, "I could
do that!"
But they didn't.
That is the difference between consumer and creator.

Which would you rather be?
Someone who hasn't created anything in years
because you're so busy consuming?
Or someone who hasn't consumed anything in years
because you're so busy creating?

Don't wait for inspiration.
Inspiration will never make the first move.
She comes only when you've shown you don't need her.
Do your work every day, no matter what.

Suspend all judgment when creating the first draft.
Just get to the end.
It's better to create something bad than nothing at all.
You can improve something bad.
You can't improve nothing.

Most of what you make will be fertilizer for the few that turn out great.
But you won't know which is which until afterward.
Keep creating as much as you can.

Creativity is a magic coin.
The more you spend, the more you have.

Don't alter your state with alcohol or drugs.
They make the mundane more interesting to you, which then makes you less interesting to others.
They make you think you're creative when you're actually boring.
Only creating makes you creative.

Embrace what's weird about you, and use it to create.
Never think you need to be normal or perfect.
Flawless people don't need to make art.

Picasso was asked if he knew what a painting was going to look like when he started it.
He said, "No, of course not. If I knew, I wouldn't bother doing it."
Don't just express yourself.
Discover yourself.
Create questions, not answers.
Explore whatever excites you most.
If you're not excited by it, your audience won't be either.

Imitate your heroes.
It's not copying because it won't be the same.
Your imitation of anything will be unrecognizably warped by your own twisted perspective.
Most creations are new combinations of existing ideas.
Originality just means hiding your sources.

Creating is a higher form of communicating.
You join the elite conversation by contributing.
You reference creations from the past to make your own
unique addition or combination.
The dialog can span centuries.

Creating is telepathy.
You speak directly to people across the world, whether days
or decades from now, connecting your mind to theirs.
You send important messages to those who can hear it.

When your creation is good enough, let it go.
Release it, so it can go out into the world, without you.
It can join the conversation, and others can improve it.

Separate creation and release.
When you've finished a work, wait a while before you
release it to the world.
By then, you're on to something new.
The public comments won't affect you, since they will
be about your past work.

Consider creating under a pseudonym.
This will help you know that criticism is not about you,
just something you made.

If you are proud of what you made, it was a success.
The less you please everyone, the more you please your fans.
Success comes not from the crowd, but from feeling proud.

Live in a city.
Cities are more conducive to creativity.
Geniuses come from cities.
It reminds you of your audience.
Ultimately, you need to connect with people, not trees.
Stay in situations where you're forced to show your work
to others.

Collect ideas in a crowd.
Create in silence and solitude.
Like your bedroom, your work space needs to be private.
This is where you dream and get naked.

Forget the view outside your window.
Focus on the view inside your head.
Instead of bringing the world in to your mind, bring
your mind out to the world.

Distribute your work as widely as you can.
Do whatever it takes to call attention to it.
Art needs an audience.
There are no unknown geniuses.

Charge money to make sure your creations are
going to people who really want them.
People don't value what's free.
Charge for their sake as much as yours.
Charge even if you don't need the money.

Incorporate a company.
Name it something you can take seriously.
You own the company, and it owns your creations.
That creates a healthy distance so the company can
demand payment for its copyrights.
It can be your guard dog and bill collector, so you can
remain a pure artist.

Keep a counterweight job.
Something effortless that covers your bills.
Something you can do a few hours per day, but
otherwise not think about.
It gives discipline and regularity to your life.
It gives deadlines and freedom to your art.

Let the deadline of death drive you.
Create until your last breath.
Let your last spark of life go into your work.
Die empty, so death takes only a corpse.

When you're gone, your work shows who you were.
Not your intentions.
Not what you took in.
Only what you put out.

Here's how to live: Don't die.

There's only one law of nature: if you survive, you win.

Be paranoid.
Avoid failure to survive.

For something to succeed, everything needs to go right.
For something to fail, only one thing needs to go wrong.

Don't try to be more right.
Just be less wrong.

Avoiding failure leads to success.
The winner is usually the one who makes the least mistakes.
This is true in investing, extreme skiing, business, flying,
and many other fields.
Win by not losing.

Most people die of cancer and heart disease.
So yes, avoid that.
But those who die from accidents die younger, losing more
years of potential life.
So try even harder to avoid accidents.
Reduce risks.

What do you want out of life?
That's hard to answer.
What don't you want?
That's easy.

More than anything, we want a lack of negatives.
A life with no pain, no injury, no regrets, and no disaster
is a good life.
It's easy to find joy in everyday things, if you can just
avoid the bad.

Bad has more power.
Insults affect you more than compliments.
Injuries affect you more than back rubs.
Poison affects you more than medicine.
A great relationship or reputation built over years
can be destroyed by one bad deed.
An otherwise perfect meal can be wrecked by one
cockroach on the plate.

But a lack of negatives is harder to talk about.
So people focus on having the upsides in life.
Instead, focus on avoiding the downsides.

Most of eating healthy is just avoiding bad food.
Most of being right is just not being wrong.
To have good people in your life, just cut out the bad ones.

Don't waste a single minute.
Life can be long if you use time wisely.
But wasting time brings death quicker.
Time is the only thing that can't be replaced.

Death reminds us that time is limited and precious.
Without death, there would be no motivation.
Death gives value to life — gives us something to lose.

Keep your eye on death.
Avoid the mistakes that end life.
Avoid the negatives that wreck life.
Avoid the time-wasting that brings death sooner.

HERE'S HOW TO LIVE:
MAKE A MILLION MISTAKES.

You learn best from your mistakes.
This is true.
So you should deliberately make as many mistakes as possible.

Try everything, all the time, expecting everything to fail.
Just make sure that you capture the lessons from each
experience.
And never make the same mistake twice.

You'll be extremely experienced.
You'll get incredibly smart.
You'll learn more lessons in a day than others learn in a year.

Deliberate mistakes are inspiring.
Trying to write a great song is hard.
Trying to write a bad song is easy and fun.
You could do it in one minute, right now.

Writers say you should quickly finish a bad first draft,
because it gets the idea out of your head and into reality,
where it can then be improved.
Live your whole life this way.
Jump into action without hesitation or worry.
You'll be faster and do more than everyone else.
What takes them a month will take you an hour, so you can
do it ten times a day.

Do what everyone says not to.
Ignore every warning so you can find out for yourself.
Learn by hands-on experience.
The more mistakes you make, the faster you learn.
Once you've made all the mistakes in a field, you're
considered an expert.

See, you only really learn when you're surprised —
when your previous idea of something was wrong.
If you're not surprised, it means the new information
fits in with what you already know.
So try to be wrong.
Try to disprove your beliefs.
Never believe something on faith.
Prove it or disprove it.
While other people have one idea that they think might work,
you will have thousands you can prove didn't work, and one
you couldn't make fail.

Just keep a log.
A mistake only counts as experience if you learn from it.
Record what you learned, and review it.
Otherwise, it was a waste.

Take on big challenges.
Start a company in Silicon Valley.
Ask investors for millions.
Audition for Hollywood movies.
Invite your dream date to dinner.
While everyone else is nervously preparing, you jump right in,
unafraid to fail.

Create predicaments.
Get into trouble.
Being desperate leads to creative solutions.

This gives you emotional stability.
No mistake will upset you.
You'll never think that a failed attempt means you're a failure.

The people devastated by failure are the ones who didn't
expect it.
They mistakenly think failure is who they are instead of the
result of one attempt.

If you're prepared for endless failures, you'll never think of yourself as a failure.

There's only one difference between a successful person and a failure.
A failure quits, which concludes the story, and earns the title.

Your growth zone is your failure zone.
Both are at the edge of your limits.
That's where you find a suitable challenge.
Aim for what will probably fail.
If you aim for what you know you can do, you're aiming too low.

It's easy to make a robot that walks.
It's hard to make a robot that can't be knocked down.
Same with people.
People who avoid mistakes are fragile, like the robot that only walks.
Your million mistakes will make you someone that can't be knocked down.

Mistakes are the fountain of youth.
The old and successful get fragile.
They think they know everything.
They over-invest in one solution.
They have only answers, not questions.
If you're never wrong, you never change.
Keep making mistakes, so you can keep changing, learning, and growing.

Share your stories from all your mistakes for the benefit of the world.
Every plane crash makes the next one less likely.

Here's how to live: Make change.

Change the world as much as you can.
All your learning and thinking is wasted if you don't
take action.
People try to explain the world, but the real point
is to change the world.

If you go through life without changing anything,
what have you done?
Just observed?!
The world doesn't need more audience.
The world needs changing.
What's broken needs fixing.
What's OK needs improving.
What's harmful needs destroying.

People dream or complain about how the world should be,
but nothing improves without action.
You have to go change things yourself.

People say the world is the way it is, and that's just how
it's going to be.
They're hopeless, complacent, or entrenched.
They expect life to stay within its current boundaries
and rules.
But all progress comes from those who ignore the boundaries,
break the rules, or make a whole new game.

Don't accept anything as-is.
Everything you encounter must change.
Preservation is your enemy.
Only dead fish go with the flow.

Think of the scientific method.
Someone proposes an idea, then others skeptically and rigorously try to disprove it.
Use this approach on the world.
Assume everything is wrong the way it is.
Doubt it and attempt to change it, to prove it's not correct.

This is how we make progress.
What fails is forgotten.
What works is called innovation.

Begin by righting what's wrong.
Look for what's ugly: ugly systems, ugly rules, ugly traditions.
Look for what bothers you.
If you can fix it, do it now.
Otherwise, aim lower until you find something you can do now.
Make it how it should be.
Don't complain.
Just make the change.

This gives you a new perspective on work.
Work is whatever you want to change.

Remove what needs to die.
Instead of fixing, destroy what was there and replace it with something better.
Sometimes you don't know what to add, but you know what to remove.

Worried you'll make things worse?
Who's to say whether the change you'll make is good or bad?
Only time will tell.
Genghis Khan killed 11% of the world's population, but he's seen as having a net-positive influence on the world in the long run.
Yet people with the best intentions can end up doing harm.

So stop judging and start changing the world any way you can.

Rearrange and remix.
That's how nature grows.
A cow is rearranged grass.
All the atoms get reused.
Every time you hear a song, watch a show, or read an idea,
think of how you'd change it or combine it with something.
Keep your tools handy to rearrange, remix, and edit what
you encounter.
Then share your alterations.

Don't worship your heroes.
Surpass them.

Changing the world includes changing yourself.
Change your beliefs, preferences, acquaintances, hobbies,
location, and lifestyle.
Your only constant habit will be looking for what to change.

Change others.
Changing minds and hearts can have more impact than
physical change.
A great speech can do the work of a thousand soldiers.

Go where there's a revolution.
That's where people are questioning old norms, and
looking for new solutions.
Creativity comes from shaking things up.
People that were left out of the old game can get in early
on the new game.

After years of doing this, you'll be ready to make
institutional change.

How?

By using the techniques of lobbyists.

Set up a company or foundation to act through.

Make institutional change anonymously from behind the
company, so your personality is not distracting the point.

Call it something generic and impossible to oppose,
like "Better World LLC".

Keep your public profile small.

Be humble and likable.

Prevent the straw man attack.

For each change you seek to make, find someone effective
to be the face for the campaign.

Let the company and its contributors make the change.

Stay behind the scenes and quietly pull the strings.

Changing culture makes revolution.

But it's not a revolution if nobody loses.

Someone will have to lose.

People will be furious.

When the bad people are mad, you're doing it right.

In the end, the highest praise of a life is to say
that person "made a difference".

Difference!

Do you hear that word?

Difference refers to what's changed.

To live a praise-worthy life, to make a difference,
you have to make change.

HERE'S HOW TO LIVE:
BALANCE EVERYTHING.

All bad things in life come from extremes.
Too much of this.
Too little of that.

When we lack balance, we're upset.
Over-worked, under-loved, over-eating, under-sleeping.
Focused on wealth, but ignoring health.
Focused on the present, but ignoring the future.

Even positive traits, when taken too far, become negative.
Someone is generous to a fault, or amusing to a fault.
Too much of a specific strength is a weakness.
If you rise to great heights in only one area, you're a
one-legged giant: easily toppled.

Notice the similarities in the physical and emotional
definitions.
Physical upset: to knock something over.
Emotional upset: to be disturbed.
Physically unstable: likely to fall.
Emotionally unstable: prone to dangerous, impulsive
behavior.
All related to a lack of balance.

When you're balanced, you're unlikely to get stressed.
You've got a stronger foundation and a resilient structure.
You can handle surprises, and make time for what's needed.

Virtue is in the balance between extremes.
Between the insecure and the egomaniac: confidence.
Between the uptight and the clown: grace.
Between the coward and the daredevil: courage.
Between selfishness and sacrifice: generosity.

So, the way to live is to balance everything.

Imagine the different aspects of your life as the spokes
in a wheel: health, wealth, intellectual, emotional, spiritual,
or however you divide it.
If any of these are lacking, it makes a lopsided, wobbly wheel,
causing you to crash.
But if you keep the parts of your life balanced, your wheel is
round, and you can roll easily.

You have different sides to your personality, with
conflicting needs.
Instead of ignoring one, make sure you balance them.
Balance time with others and time alone.
Balance your need for stability with your need for surprise.
Balance input and output, consumption and creation,
stability and adventure, body and spirit.
Your opposing needs become each other's remedy.

Work more on your weaknesses.
Someone who's rich but fat has different needs than
someone who's fit but broke.
Remember the spokes of the wheel.

The best tool for a balanced life is the clock.
Like a hunter's dog, the clock will be your best ally.
It will guard you, keep your impulses in check, and protect
what's important to you.

Schedule everything to ensure balance of your time and effort.
Scheduling prevents procrastination, distraction, and
obsession.
A schedule makes you act according to the goals of your
highest self, not your passing mood.

Schedule quality time with dear friends.
Schedule preventative health checkups.

Schedule focused time to learn.
Schedule each aspect of your life, ignoring none.
List what makes you happy and fulfilled, then schedule those
things into your year.

The balanced schedule protects you from hurting yourself,
from getting overwhelmed and ignoring important needs.
You won't over-work, over-play, or over-indulge.

Even creative work needs scheduling.
The greatest writers and artists didn't wait for inspiration.
They kept a strict daily schedule for creating their art.
A routine triggers inspiration because your mind and body
learn that ideas emerge at that time.
The world's greatest achievements were squeezed into
existence by deadlines.

Set an alarm to start and stop on time.
Obey your schedule, no matter how you feel.
Schedule every hour of your day.
Distraction steals what's not locked down.

Once you're living a balanced life, find new layers.
The wheel has infinite spokes.

Balance your needs versus the needs of others.

Balance your knowledge.
Read books on core subjects you know nothing about.

Balance your political opinion.
Talk with smart people in the opposite camp until you're not
opposite anymore.

Balance the abilities of your body.
Improve your flexibility, strength, coordination, and ability to
perform different types of movements.

Balance two languages.
A second language is one of the best things for your brain,
and can add a new type of balance, like living half the year
in another culture, speaking only your other language.

Balance your response to situations.
Do you tend to change yourself, change the environment,
or change nothing and leave?
Find which you do too much and which you don't do enough,
then rebalance.

Finally, balance the world.
Help lift up those who have been pushed down.
Counterbalance sexism, racism, and religious discrimination.
Feed the hungry.
Balance justice.
Balance human nature.

By balancing everything in your life, you postpone nothing.
You won't postpone happiness, dreams, love, or expression.
You could die happy at any time.

Balancing everything is how to live.

Conclusion

Is this a duck or bunny?

No. This is a duck and bunny.

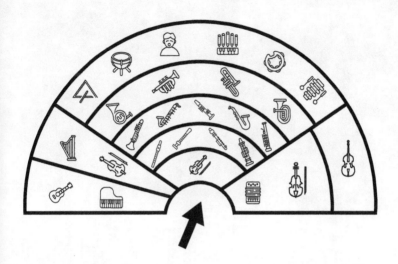

This is an orchestra.

You are the composer and conductor.

About the Author

If you want to know more about me or my work, go to **sive.rs**. It's all there.

Any questions, go to **sive.rs/contact** to email me.

— Derek

Books by Derek Sivers

Anything You Want
40 lessons for a new kind of entrepreneur
sive.rs/a

Your Music and People
creative and considerate fame
sive.rs/m

Hell Yeah or No
what's worth doing
sive.rs/n

How to Live
27 conflicting answers and one weird conclusion
sive.rs/h

Printed in the USA
CPSIA information can be obtained
at www.ICGtesting.com
CBHW021833091024
15572CB00015B/1010

9 781991 152336